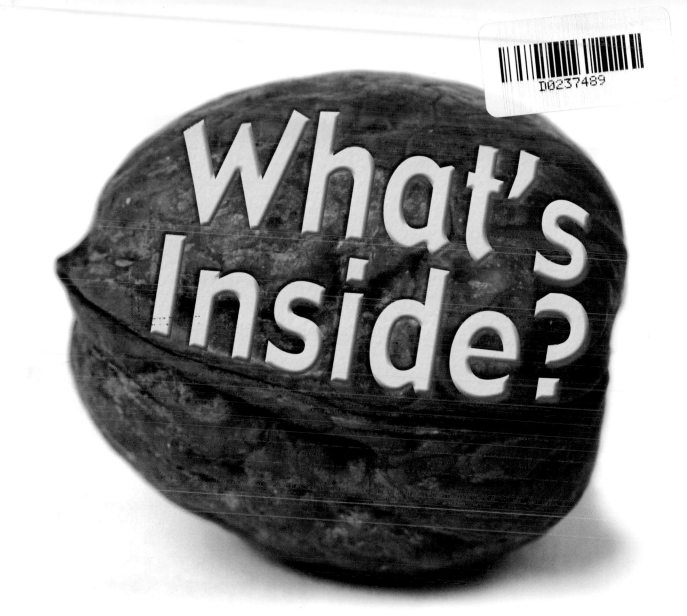

What's Inside?

Written by Monica Hughes

Collins

What's inside this pod?

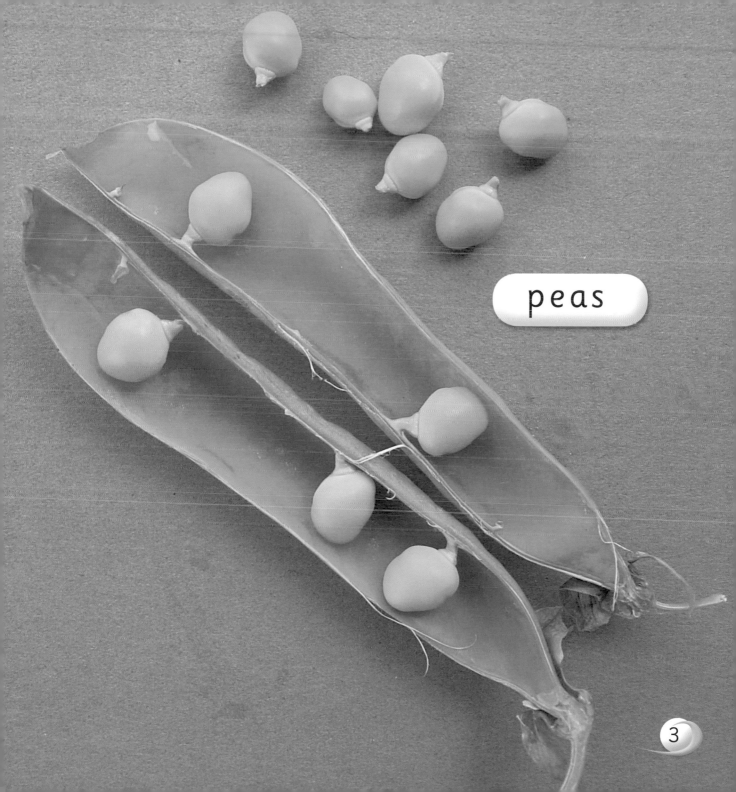

peas

3

What's inside this nut?

a walnut

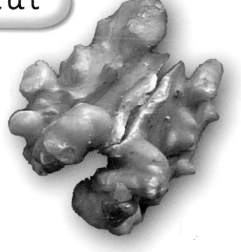

What's inside this pupa?

a butterfly

What's inside this hive?

bees

What's inside this egg?

a turtle

11

What's inside you and me?

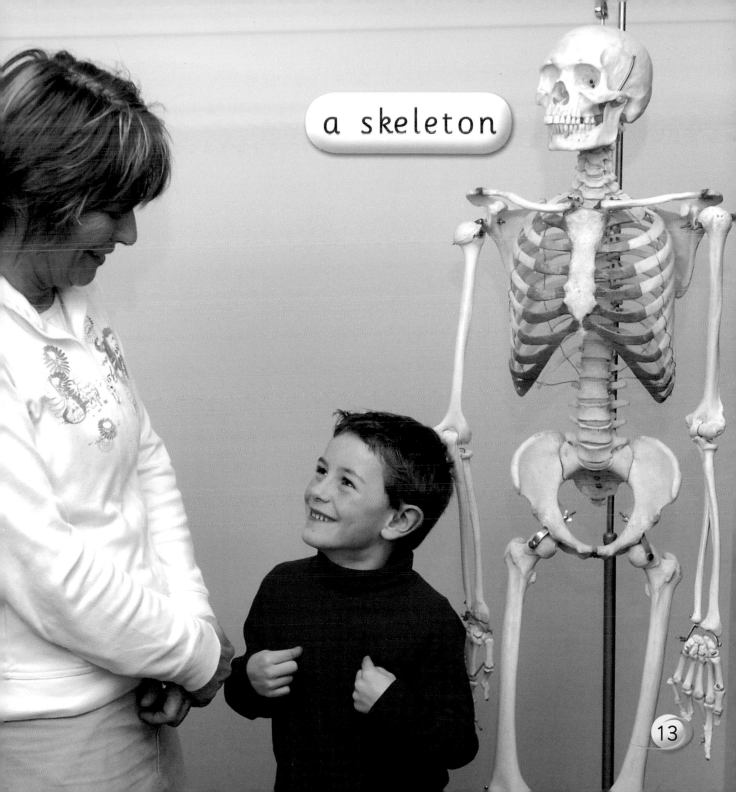

a skeleton

13

What's inside?

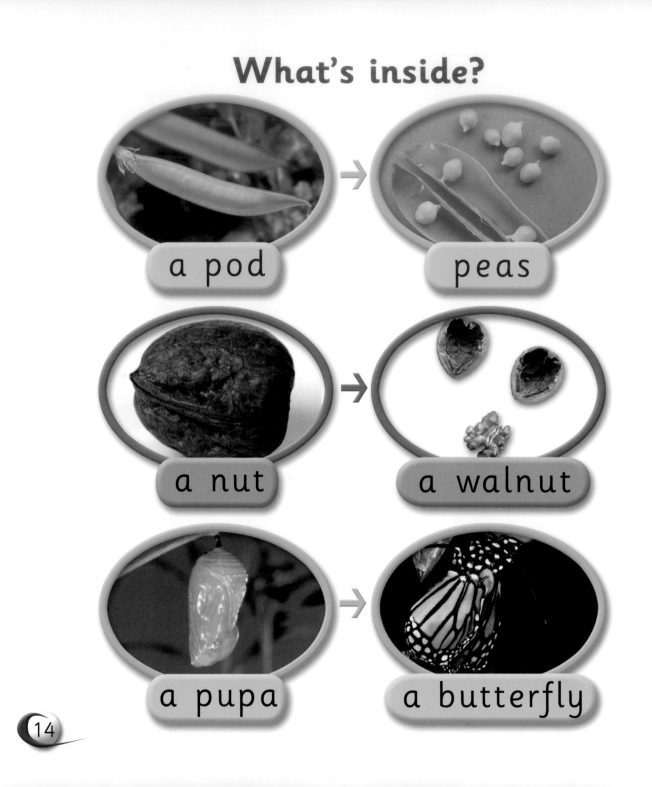

a pod → peas

a nut → a walnut

a pupa → a butterfly

a hive → bees

an egg → a turtle

you and me → a skeleton

Ideas for reading

Written by Clare Dowdall, PhD
Lecturer and Primary Literacy Consultant

Learning objectives: To understand terms about books (cover, title, label); to read letters that represent sounds; to read on sight familiar words; to make collections of personal interest words relating to topics; to use talk to organise, sequence and clarify thinking.

Curriculum links: Knowledge and understanding of the world: identify features of living things and objects

High frequency words: is, in, this, you, and, me

Interest words: pod, inside, pea, nut, walnut, pupa, butterfly, hive, bees, egg, turtle, skeleton

Word count: 35

Getting started

- Look at the cover together. Find *Inside* on the front cover. Look at it and read it together. Prompt the children to find the small words *in* and *side.* Ask what *inside* means (what is inside your pencil case/sandwich?).
- Look at the photograph on the front cover. What is the photo of? What do the children think is 'inside' it?
- Ask the children to find the different parts of the book, for example, the front cover, the back cover, the title or a label. Focus on the term 'label', and look for labels in the classroom. Explain that labels name things.
- Walk through the book together, looking at the pages. For each left hand page, ask children to discuss what's inside the image. Introduce new words (e.g. *pod, walnut, pupa*) if the children do not know them.

Reading and responding

- Ask the children to read the book independently and aloud up to p13. Observe, prompt and praise use of fingers, one-to-one matching, and fluent reading of the repeated text.
- Encourage children to use their phonic knowledge when tackling new words.
- Ask the children to look at pp14-15, and ask them to recap what is inside what, referring to the labels underneath the pictures.